Autobiography of Horse

Autobiography of Horse

A POEM

Jenifer Sang Eun Park

GAUDY BOY

Published by Gaudy Boy LLC,
an imprint of Singapore Unbound
www.singaporeunbound.org/gaudyboy
New York

For more information on ordering books, contact jkoh@singaporeunbound.org.

ISBN 978-0-9828142-4-6

Cover design by Flora Chan
Interior design by Christina Newhard
Proofread by Cindy Hochman of "100 Proof" Copyediting Services

What happened, as we were traversing the
whole heaven, is that the imagination lost its power to
sustain us. It has the strength of reality or none at all.

WALLACE STEVENS
"The Noble Rider and the Sound of Words"

For Sharonee and Jonathan

Autobiography of Horse

In 12th-century Kenil Cunil, the most remote part of Ulster Ireland, a king is inaugurated through the slaughter and ceremonial consumption of a mare. The appointed mare must be as white as a bleached skull. Once the mare is identified, she's led to the center of the crowd and waits for the new king to confess humility by crawling to her on all fours. By rephrasing his body, the king submits himself as a beast to another beast. After the initial transaction is complete, the white mare is cut into pieces and boiled in a large cauldron. From the stewing broth a bath is prepared for the king. The king sits in the cauldron and is served chunks of the mare's flesh. Members of the community stand around the cauldron to share the flesh with the king. Later, the king is required to drink the broth by lapping it up with his mouth. At this moment the transfer is complete.

Two white mares in a field, equally formidable and equally beautiful. Each contemplates: Which of us will be taken for our blood and meat? Which will be good enough for the next king?

Horse: Do you remember the feeling of feeling?
Me: Sometimes.
H: What color are my eyes?
M: All the colors.
H: Are they beautiful?
M: No. They make me nervous.
H: When was the last time you had a good sleep?
M: It's difficult to remember.
H: It's difficult to remember.
M: It's difficult to remember.

I ate the horse years ago and it still hasn't left my body. A serving of horse is 28g of protein, 6g of fat, 5mg of iron, 55mg of sodium, 65mg of cholesterol, and a total of 175 calories. A serving of horse has 25% less fat, 27% less sodium, and 30% less cholesterol than ground beef. Horsemeat is low in saturated fats, rich in polyunsaturated fats, and proven to lower cholesterol. I watch the next horse butcher itself. And the next. The horse lives as a forever-cadaver.

Though previously endangered, the horse of Jeju-do, an island located in the Korea Strait, is still considered a delicacy. Due to its lean profile, the Jeju horse is more tender and flavorful when eaten raw. Once the meat is pulled from the stocky rectangular frame, it's tossed in sesame oil for a light tartare, placed on a nub of rice, or positioned in a ring of thick slices on a decorated plate. Horsemeat, however, isn't the only use of the Jeju horse: its soul is extracted and manufactured into creams and oils for beauty products and its bones are ground up and sold as pills for the treatment of arthritis and bone diseases.

Ancient Patagonian Indians extract the stomach of a mare to hold a baby. Once the soft packet of human flesh enters the sinewy stomach, a spiritual osmosis occurs. Encased in the wet and still-warm envelope of her stomach, the child is imbued with the qualities of the horse. Under a more vigorous procedure, the neck, body, and legs of the horse are lassoed. Members of the tribe distribute themselves across each end of the lasso to upturn and steady the horse. As soon as the horse slows her breathing, the father of the child slits the mare from the neck down. After the heart and innards are removed, the baby is placed in the cavity. The goal is to keep the animal stuttering until the child is placed inside his secondary womb. If achieved, the Patagonian Indians believe they ensure the child's destiny as a superior horseman. The remainder of the mare is prepared for a feast and the community joins to savor the sum.

A 150g bottle of Jeju Horse Bone Pills sells for $48.32. A 50ml container of Jeju Horse Oil Cream sells for $47.90. The Horse Oil Soothing Gel Cream is $12.84. And the luxurious Jeju Horse Placenta & Oil Natural Facial Cream is an even $124.00. Some of us are ingenious cannibals.

The night before my inauguration as king of Kenil Cunil, I'll paint every white mare black. "See," I'll say when they look for the white mare. "She's gone and there are none." On inauguration day, I'll walk to the center and ask to be cut and boiled into a broth. "Cook me," I'll say, "then gather the black mares and bathe them in my soup. Feed them my flesh."

I learned long ago how futile it is to resist what we feel. Hence, control lies in the absence of resistance. Impatient, I waited. Silent, I spoke. Mutable, I steadied. In the wait, the horse shed two legs and slipped through a seam in the mirror. The horse became that crucial bite—the beginning of a story gone awry.

A chain of white mares standing in pools of black-red-black chewing.

A white mare waits

The Red Horse
wears a saddle
made of my bones
slings my limp casing
over his back
takes me to a hill
rears to drop me.
My eyes fall out
& tumble
into my mouth.
He pours gasoline
over me
& lights the night.

In the Omak Suicide Race, horses and their riders have 50 feet to rush, then sprint, 500 yards down Suicide Hill, a rise grinning with a 60-degree slope. After successfully sprinting down the hill, the horse and rider must cross the Okanogan River. After this sloppy 50-yard swim, the horse and rider climb out to speed toward the finish line. Excited spectators eagerly greet the drenched and dirty survivors. Some horses fall and roll to the bottom of the hill or, unable to grasp their breath or footing, sink and disappear into the river. Other horses die during training, in practice trials, or after completing the race. Though the race began in 1935, only 21 deaths have been accounted for in the last 25 years.

My parents used to take us to Wyoming, where we'd ride old horses along a worn path. "Wear jeans and covered shoes," I'd remind everyone. I was always the first to run out of the car. To pat the horse's face was to touch something godly.

In 344 BC Macedonia, a bullish black horse was offered to Alexander the Great's father, King Philip II. Unable to tame the horse himself, the king watched disapprovingly as his men took turns trying to calm the massive horse. From a short distance, 13-year-old Alexander observed these attempts and waged 13 talents against his father for the opportunity to tame and keep the horse. Humored, the king acquiesced. In one swift exchange, Alexander straddled the horse and named him *Bucephalus*.

Defenders of the Omak Suicide Race argue that the race is the ultimate demonstration of the animal and human working in complete unity. In order to display such ostentatious athleticism, the horse and rider must fuse into a single harmonious unit. What they fail to mention is that unity requires a loss from both parties. That the rider is the one being ridden. That the horse will die, but the rider won't. That the horse will never really die.

Since 1980, runners and riders on horseback have gathered to race on a scenic 22-mile stretch in Llanwrtyd Wells for the annual Man versus Horse Marathon. Though now an established event, the race began in jest. Gordon Green, a pub owner, overheard a couple of patrons discussing theories of the differential endurance between the horse and man. A patron hypothesized that over a long distance, a man can beat a horse in a race. Intrigued, Green organized the first Man versus Horse Marathon. Hundreds of individuals tested their bodies against the horse. The horse, however, is known for being a particularly difficult opponent. It was on the 25th anniversary of the race that a human, Huw Lobb, first beat the horse. "Finally, finally!" the town yelled.

Many horse enthusiasts claim Alexander to be the first horse whisperer because he understood the horse's capacity for fear. Afraid of his own shadow, Bucephalus nervously trotted around the large puddle cast onto the ground. Alexander cupped Bucephalus's face, turned him toward the sun, and mounted the golden black smokestack. On Bucephalus's neck, Alexander hung a pendant embossed with the heads of Gorgons. Around Bucephalus's neck, Alexander hung his eyes.

We politely followed the guide and his horse in a single line. Horse-butt to horse-head at a leisurely pace. I wanted so badly to kick the horse with my heels. To make it gallop. To feel it breathe hard under me. I was never brave enough and it'd take us a few hours to circle back to the stable. When I got off the horse, I marveled at the numbness in my legs. As the car turned out of the stable, I rolled down the window to tell my horse goodbye. "Spaghetti legs, spaghetti legs," I said on our way back home. Later I would learn that bravery can come out of loss. That the horse has been galloping under me for years.

A camera is attached to the helmet of a rider. A young white horse. The race begins. Whipping. Down the hill they go. Shaking, yelling. The descent. The heartbeats. They plunge into the river. Riders fall from horses. Horses twist out into the periphery. Whipping. Water on the lens. Water plugging nostrils. The horse pushes forward. Whipping. They climb out. The added weight of water. The added weight of breathlessness. Whipping. They sprint. The shaking. The lens occluded by rising dust. The panting and throbbing. The strain of each push forward. The horse is not here. The horse crossed the finish line before I even started.

It's not certain whether or not Bucephalus died from wounds delivered at the Battle of Hydaspes. It is certain, however, that in the exact moment Bucephalus passed, Alexander felt his feet loosen from the earth. The massive coffin cast a larger shadow, and in that shadow Alexander stood, motionless and blind.

Equine self-mutilation syndrome is a condition involving a repetitive and seemingly dysfunctional sequence of movements. An otherwise normal horse could develop a habit of biting herself from flank to shoulder to chest. Another otherwise normal horse could start shaking her head repeatedly, as if to say *no no no* to whatever distresses her. Though self-injurious, "the performance of a stereotypy, no matter what the initial precipitating cause, is self-rewarding." Stereotypies have been associated with a variety of factors, such as excitement, stress, boredom, and the scent of poop or piss.

A few years ago I developed the habit of grinding my teeth. A committee would call it *bruxism*. My mom noticed this when we shared a hotel room in Colma. "You grind your teeth," she said as we ate breakfast. I stopped eating and looked at her. I didn't know what it sounded like, so I looked it up. A woman recorded her husband grinding his teeth in his sleep. It is the worst sound a human can make.

I sit in front of a building and watch who opens the door for strangers. "She is nice," I say, when she extends her arm to keep the door pried open. She is not a horse. "He is nice," I say, when he opens the door for others before he walks in. He is not a horse. I can't stop.

Colma, a short BART ride from San Francisco, is popularly known as the "City of Souls." With most of its land dedicated to cemeteries, the population of the dead exceeds the town's living population. I know exactly what it feels like to live among the dead. My job is to talk to the dead. My job is to undo the living.

Major was a horse tired of life. For Major, the inclination for self-mutilation evolved into attempts to end. From the railway, a dead lighthouse. Past the billets of azaleas, the trestle bridge. Here, Major attempted for the first time. Though he understood the physics of falling, he tripped and caught his hind legs on the trestle's latticework. He hung like a hinged apple until someone saw the black mass curling and uncurling like a beckoning finger. It took two hours to lower Major into the river and return him to his stall.

Sometimes I hear so many hooves, I lose my way back home.

Major tried again. He was found in his stall with his halter wound around his throat. He was half dead, with a wrecked blood vessel in his neck. They brought him back again. To leave and be brought back is considered to be lucky. Luck is nothing but an empty canteen in a winding trail of escapes and returns.

In my teeth is a city of souls, scratching to escape and neigh. There are no known causes for bruxism, but many cite stress as a factor. "Did I grind my teeth last night?" I ask my partner. "Was it bad?" I try to do it when I'm awake and I fail. The pressure required to mill molars against each other for even the slightest audibility is too difficult to reenact. I floss out bones and watch histories trample out. I ate too many horses on my way here.

In a photo, the body of a horse with a malignant tumor is cut for wolf feed. Hung from the neck, the body hangs on a scaffold of three wooden poles peaked into a tripod. The horse's rigid head faces west. A bloated tongue limps out of his mouth. Behind the hanging horse is a parched tree and behind this tree is a ditched school bus. Below, a man wearing glasses; a brown tank top; and a pair of light jeans, hole at the knee, bends to strip the meat from the hindquarters. Beside him, a wooden box where the cuts of meat will be preserved. The mane cascades the same shade of dusty blond as the man's ponytail. If the photo were cropped, it'd be a still of a rearing stallion. The horse's eyes are shut for the pleasure of being carved for another animal.

I split my own body to carry the horse inside me. I lasso my appendages and stretch them onto stakes. I pull the blade from my neck down. I see my cavity stuttering. For each inhalation I blame myself.

Rearing

The man carving meat from the horse for his wolves doesn't know that what hangs above him is the horse of him hanging. You can see other versions of the self if the mirror is used properly.

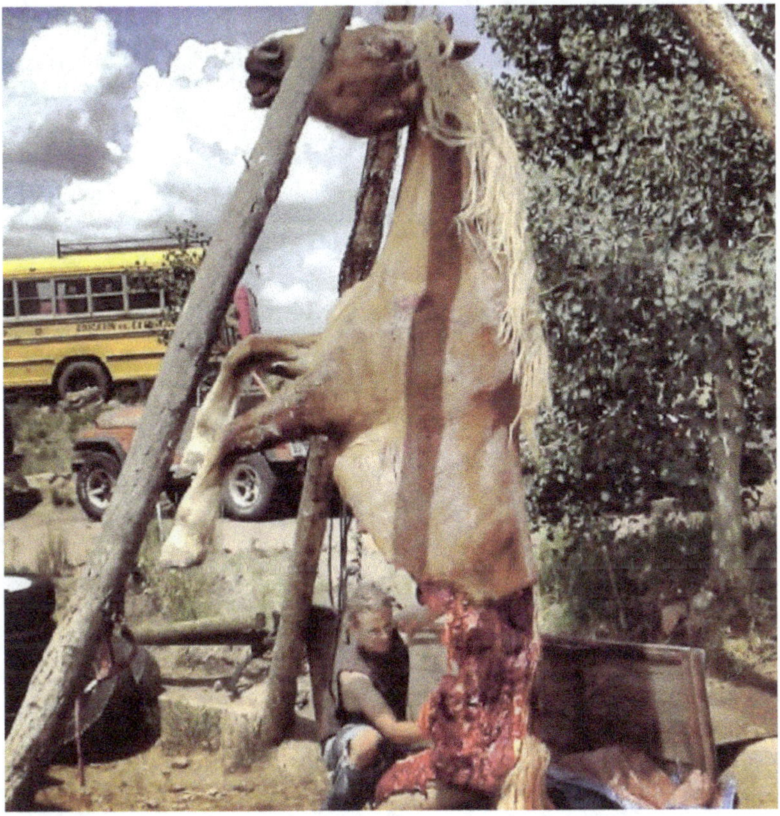

Feed

H: What did you do today?

M: I sat in front of my bowl of oatmeal & thought of burning you.

H: Do you think I want this?

M: No.

H: What are my bones made of?

M: An alphabet that hates me.

H: You made me like this.

M: You made me like this.

According to Korean superstition, a "weak" person is more likely to be inhabited by a spirit than a person of "stronger character." And in Korean, 말, pronounced *mahl,* means "horse." 말 also means "word," "speech," and "utterance." This is some kind of destiny.

I crushed hard in the beginning. The horse was an answer to each prompt. In the horse's body, I saw the possibilities of my own body. In the horse's past, I saw my own past. The horse understood me and I wanted to share this oblivion. There was no human to share it with. I shared a mirror with the horse.

Some explanations:

1. I just think horses are cool.
2. I was tired of seeing the sky in your eyes.
3. At the end there was a question mark.
4. I got lost on my way home.
5. The mirror needed fixing.
6. Because the past is more uncertain than the future.
7. My body is too small for my body.
8. No other mask seemed to fit.
9. I was jealous.
10. I shit my heart out & needed a replacement.
11. I was playing the longest game of hide-and-seek.
12. I came upon a fortress & the door was locked.
13. I was experimenting with renewable energy sources.
14. My grandma is a horse.
15. My horse is not my grandma.
16. I am the Judas horse.

Like the horse's reflection, Reiter Mahl dissolves and vanishes into the eye. Mahl is known to be the most mysterious and evasive equine enthusiast, historian, and researcher of this century. In his most personal work, *As a Rider,* Mahl recounts his childhood spent on a ranch. Though this work opens a private door to Mahl's extensive knowledge of equine matters, he does not provide the name of the ranch or any other identifying locators. Nor does he provide any names, except the names of his favorite horses, Anastasia and Sandman. And though there are no records of his date of birth or location of birth, it is widely believed that Mahl is still alive and still sharing his work. In most cases, it's the horse inside us that keeps us alive.

A friend asks if I want to see a horse. "She has a horse at her ranch. We can drive up there anytime." With false exuberance, I say, "Yes, of course!" I reply in the way the obsession taught me. This meeting will never happen. "Not today. I'm not feeling well." Or, "Maybe this weekend? I have work to do today." I'm afraid of looking into the horse's eyes and finding in that single gaze the meaning of both hatred and love.

I have correspondents, though I call them my horse angels. You trip and tell your friends, colleagues, and family, "I've fallen in love with the horse. It's all I can think and write about." This is when people give you things imprinted with the horse—a book, a mug, a poster, a sticker, a shot glass, a stuffed horse, etc.—you accept them and say, "Thank you, thank you!" This is when you go to the thrift shop and buy an ill-fitting T-shirt with a mule on it. This is when you buy a contraption that when affixed to your bicycle will mimic the sound of a trotting horse. And when it doesn't arrive, you complain only minimally and check the mailbox periodically. This is when a friend, in an attempt to cheer you up, agrees to take you to a ranch in the middle of the night because "there are horses" and you shrug. Each gift is another device for torture.

The Red Horse
doesn't sleep
in a stall
or a bed
but in a shoebox
& the spine
of a book
or me.

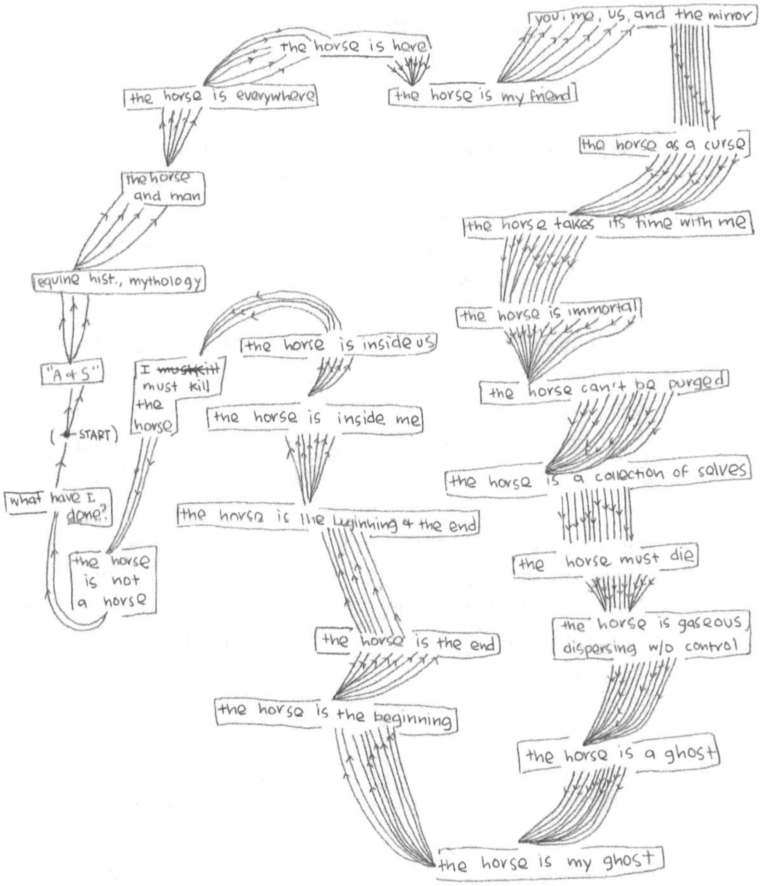

A timeline

I put on a white coat and diagnose myself with made-up maladies. I'm concerned with speaking procedurally and matter-of-factly. To be a doctor means to have the intent to heal. This puts me on the other side of the mirror. What I see is both enough and emptying. I assign myself symptoms of Critical Obsession, Sympathetic Spontaneous Combustion, Latent Retrieval Learning, Death Dissonance, and Para-Psyche. I give myself these things because it makes me sick with comprehension.

horse horse

horse horse

horse why horse

Horse horse horse

A critical obsession is one that endures long enough to change the individual's core perception values. This infection can be felt immediately and explicitly, or slowly and implicitly. There are countless ways an obsession infects the consciousness of an individual, but immediate attention should be paid to the initial implosion. Though variations also exist within these parameters, the onset of a critical obsession is evident in a momentous implosion that viscerally conflicts with the self. This implosion primarily affects the individual's emotional-motor skills, present-tense cognition, and reality-perception. The implosion seeps deeply and thoroughly, much like an exodus of locusts.

To think of the image beyond one's normal responsibilities is, according to some subjects, a "curse." All processed subjects later perceive this "curse" as a self-inflicted, necessary event for their completion. To highlight this phenomenon is an excerpt from the testimony completed by our core subject approximately mid-process:

> It isn't possible to be simple. Sandman, when I met you I was hiding under a cloak. I was unhappy and you were there to meet me for coffee and scones at a café I'd never heard of before. We had the same assignment. I wrote in front of you, and later, for you. I made Anastasia. *Anastasia was real. She was pulled apart by tractors. She drowned herself. She starved herself. A .22 caliber to the head.* I make it all up so I can be made. Killing her was necessary. I grey the want and need.
>
> I didn't mean to hurt you if that's what you're thinking. I'm too "something-something" for that.
>
> Sometimes it's easy to see Anastasia on a hill enjoying the shade of a large tree. She's quiet and still. I don't even know what she looks like in motion. But you, Sandman, you're different. You're always moving. I scroll into the future and find you mid-sentence. I turn to see if you're behind me. You're not there. You used to be. You used To Be. I face forward, only to see you on a horizon so far my eyes water from the strain of searching. I forget what I'm doing. Anastasia respected me because she was me. You, Sandman, are the tractors. Gasoline and metal. I wrote so you could kill me or I

wrote in the killing of me to kill you. In either situation, there was an *is* or there is a *was*. And falling is the same as rising. Before the horses. During the horses. When the horses. In the horses. But what of the after?

I see now the opportunities to be an animal, an inanimate object, a reality, a sentence. It is exactly what it seems—a question.

Before the light dims, the horse across the room winks and turns his head. The horse sips on an Old Fashioned. The horse tells you a story. Beneath this story is a heritage of loss. Nothing is uncovered except the act of uncovering. Nothing can make "sense" in such lighting. One can write more and more. One can attempt to "write it out," as if there were a limited amount of words and these words can be purged through continual work until one arrives at this magical number. None of this works. This is how to think like a horse horse horse when writing.

There is no philosophy except the one you believe when you're a lone horse. There is no philosopher except the soldier who died because his horse failed to outrun the bullets or arrows or spears or pikes. I'm unmarried to the history of a real field. This field is a corner in the mind of the unreal. I don't know what is real or what will be real. What will be real is scarier to imagine than what is real.

The horses arrive to eat me. I let them chew me. I say, "Welcome to the dinner show. I've been waiting. I had to take myself out of the fridge, so excuse the cold." I say, "Enjoy the meal. I've been baking for long enough."

horse horse the subject's horse thinking horse horse horse opportunities horse perception horse limited horse duress horse nonlinear horse web horse horse process horse horse devolves horse horse horse horse acuity horse slanted horse creation horse horse horse horse beyond horse experience horse horse horse horse horse horse horse horse horse horse horse horse horse horse horse horse horse horse manifests horse

horse horse horse horse horse horse horse horse lives horse haunt horse

horse haunt horse

The Red Horse
drinks whiskey
out of Styrofoam cups
gets high
into the night
sings me songs
I can't untie
combs my hair
until it falls out
tells me I'm the ugliest
thing he's ever seen
tells me I'm the most
beautiful when I'm wrong
is the finger
I put in my mouth
when I bend over
the toilet.

Tommy Burns, a.k.a. Timmy Robert Ray, killed horses for a living. He was one of the best in the business. When he made his rounds on the circuit, spectators would mutter, "Shh, the Sandman's coming. Shh, the Sandman's here." In each racehorse and show horse is a titan holding a bag of money called "insurance." Sandman the Man killed racehorses to help owners collect the sum. He charged $5,000 for 10 minutes of work. In 10 years, he knocked off more than a dozen horses with his method of choice, death by electrocution. A split electrical cord rigged with alligator clips. One clip to the anus and another to an ear. Once the clips were affixed, he stood back and plugged in the cord. In a single spastic moment, the racehorse would drop dead. To ensure the collection of insurance, the horse must be pronounced dead by accident or illness. Electrocution is particularly effective because it can be disguised as colic in an autopsy. Electrocution is quick and clean. Electrocution is a hush, hushed further by paperwork. "Shh, the Sandman's coming. Shh, the Sandman's here. He's here."

. . . two days before Anastasia leapt from the cliff to drown I brought water to her in a large ceramic bowl. The bowl, covered in tiny poppies lazily and haphazardly painted, was part of a china set purchased from an older woman three miles east of the ranch. When I held the bowl under her mouth, I suddenly became very thirsty. Anastasia stopped, leaving me a cupful of water. I tilted the bowl and drank. She nuzzled me, though she knew two days later she'd jump from the cliff because she was still thirsty.

—RM, As a Rider

Sandman the Man excelled in the business of killing because he knew no racehorse knows the smell of money. No racehorse knows their estimated stud fee or the extent of their racing career earnings. It was easy to do work that didn't need to be explained. To Sandman the Man, it was all about money. Put the horse to sleep and collect. Put the horse to sleep and collect. This horse. Then that horse. Then this horse. And another.

Sandman the Man was caught on the stormy night of the Streetwise attempt. He was ordered to break the leg of Streetwise, a show jumper, in order to corroborate the following story for the insurance claim: "Streetwise slipped in the rain and broke his leg. He was in so much pain, he had to be euthanized." While Sandman the Man steadied Streetwise, his assistant, Harlow Arlie, swung a crowbar to break the horse's right leg. The leg snapped, and in shock, Streetwise ran out of the stable. Sandman the Man and Mr. Arlie desperately trailed behind Streetwise, calling his name, half concerned for the job and half concerned for the horse. Local officials were notified of a possible Sandman the Man killing and were in the vicinity of the stable. Sandman the Man was caught. In most reports, Sandman the Man expresses guilt and remorse. In other reports, he is just a man trying to make a living. In fewer reports, he is depicted as a charming, likable man who grew up poor, ran away at 15, saved enough to buy a Cadillac, rescued a three-legged cat, and took care of three dogs.

I met with a psychiatrist a few times. She was interested enough. She provided scientific explanations. This was what I wanted. Pragmatism in a stampede of abstractions. She told me about spectrums, bodily deficiencies, and genetics. She told me her husband is a history professor and that he presented something on Sylvia Plath. She told me about writers and depression. I did not turn my psychiatrist into a horse. She became a horseshoe I threw into the sea.

Interested in the peculiarities of equinophobia, I imagined the life of a boy named George. George has periodic nightmares of horses trampling his body. After school, George masturbates to the children's cartoon *My Little Pony.* When he's 26, he'll kill himself.

Sandman the Man meets Sandman the Horse. Sandman the Horse takes Sandman the Man up a hill. Sandman the Horse rears. Sandman the Man feels Sandman the Horse's body tighten under him. Sandman the Man holds on, though he doesn't know where they're going. I know exactly where they're going. They gallop away. Am I guiltier than Sandman the Man? Is it because I won't let the horse die? Who is the greater beast of burden?

The Red Horse
follows me to the clinic.
I follow him out.

In the Wikipedia entry for "Equinophobia," Kansas City Chiefs safety Eric Berry is the first name listed under "notable people suffering from equinophobia." Berry has been recorded multiple times vocalizing, and sometimes reacting physically to, his fear of Warpaint, the Chiefs' mascot. After each home game touchdown, Warpaint takes a victory lap around the field with his rider, Susie. "I don't fuck with that horse," Berry says, pacing nervously on the sidelines. In a brief NFL Films documentary, Berry admits he was not averse to horses until he realized actual horses are unlike the fanciful renditions caricatured in *My Little Pony.* Owing to this realization and having been emotionally bludgeoned by an unfortunate incident at a petting zoo, Berry developed equinophobia.

"Do you have a history of self-harm? When was the last time you thought about these things?" What I want to explain to the committee is that there's no time. More specifically, in here there's no time. Instead, I move away from the truth. I loosen myself for the presentation. I smile. She gives me material. A brochure. A chart. A drawing. I stuff them into my bag and smile again. Don't you understand that I know all of this? Don't you understand that I'll use this as fodder for the fire? Don't you understand I'm in danger? I see her doing this a few times a day. I see her making more copies. I see her filling the manila folder with more brochures, more charts, more drawings. This is her job. We all have jobs.

George is a boy who prefers sucking on wrappers to eating the candy. When no one's looking, he unwraps the candy, discards the candy, and crumples the wrapper into his mouth. If the wrapper is made of either plastic or foil, he savors it until the printed colors run off. If the wrapper is made of paper, he lets it dissolve in his mouth. He chews on the wrapper only when he's anxious. When he's not anxious, he lets the wrapper blanket his tongue. / George is afraid of horses. So much so, he has nightmares of horses stampeding through his room and trampling his body. He hears his bones breaking. He hears his kidneys exploding. He hears his heart squishing. The wet cracks white and red. He is convinced a neigh, no matter the volume, is the sound of killing. / George is a good kid. He gets good grades. He doesn't stay out past nine. He reads a lot of books. George has many friends. / George masturbates to the children's cartoon *My Little Pony* once after school and once more before he goes to sleep. / George is an only child. / The first time George kissed a girl, he was eating Cheetos. / When George sees his semen, he cries. /

to consider "the conveyance of an obsession that's devolved into parenthetical thinking." It's endangered living. Each sentence I begin is another temptation to begin with the I. I want to avoid this. I want to kill this. I am not here. I am not. I am. I don't want. I don't need. I hate. There's so much room for mistake.

I met the horse between pages, then in the spine of the book. This horse grew into a person. This person grew into a horse. The only difference between a horse and a human is two additional legs. This isn't a curse. It's a premonition of our evolutional failures.

Before time there was space and before space was the horse. In this world, we are objects of pleasure to an animal. In this world, we end from our lack of beginnings.

I have to know how to make money in order to have a horse. IDK what kind of horse I want, but I do want a horse with a story. I want a horse that wants to be rescued from the horse

The last horse I saw had blue eyes. This is an atypical trait of the horse. I don't know if this is true. I don't know much about horses. This doesn't take a lot to admit. This is what makes an obsession humanizing. This is what makes an obsession humiliating. This is what makes an obsession both acceptable and unacceptable. This is what makes my obsession worthy.

I know I wasn't born to be obsessed with the horse. I know I wasn't born to be a switchblade in the hand of a child.

I spend this time alone. I spend it as an

investment. I realize no horse knows I'm writing about the horse. We can't meet in the place of words and pages. This is an inherent problem I find in whatever I decide to write. Words are too mutable to be sturdy bridges. Curiously, this lack of constancy is what interests me in writing neigh neigh neigh though no horse can hear this neigh neigh neigh or even understand this neigh neigh neigh or even hear this neigh neigh neigh as mimicry of their own neigh neigh neigh.

Horse horse horse

It's necessary to recommend subjects with horse horse horse horse experience as isolated events, thusly concluding that horse subjects resist similar applications. However, horse horse the example of horse is peculiarly horse eclipsing horse. The following are notes from an extensive examination on the subject posthumously identified as horse:

horse the horse horse horse horse horse horse horse horse horse horse horse story horse horse horse horse horse horse horse horse is horse horse horse horse autonomous horse

horse horse horse horse horse horse horse
horse horse horse horse horse horse horse
horse horse horse horse horse horse horse
horse horse horse horse horse horse horse
horse horse horse horse horse horse horse
horse horse horse horse horse horse horse
horse horse horse horse horse horse horse
horse horse horse horse horse horse horse
horse horse horse horse horse horse horse
horse horse horse horse horse horse horse
horse horse horse horse horse horse horse
horse horse horse horse horse horse horse
horse horse horse horse horse horse horse
horse horse horse horse

In his locker are the usual items: textbooks, pencils, notebooks, folders, and a calculator. According to George, the most enjoyable part of homework is the act of turning it in. He enjoys that brief process of unzipping his backpack, pulling out his homework folder, gently tugging the homework assignment from the folder's pocket, and looking into the teacher's eyes as he holds the assignment up. / The first time George tried beer was the weekend his parents left for a cruise. His parents left with Deena's parents. Deena is a girl George likes. Deena rang the doorbell with her left elbow, her tiny hands nervously wrapped around a six-pack. Deena's older brother agreed to buy her beer as long as she promised not to tell their parents about getting his girlfriend pregnant. George opened the door, his hands clutching a bag of Cheetos. / George's parents believe their son is a pragmatic and wholesome boy. When George learned how to ride his bicycle, he wore his helmet and reimagined mailboxes as traffic lights. Once he spotted a mailbox in the distance, he anticipated its color—yellow, red, or green. Depending on the color he'd slow down and come to a complete stop or continue riding past the mailbox. Sometimes he imagined the mailbox at its last seconds of greenness. In these situations he sped as fast as he could, his legs pushing and pushing until he passed the mailbox right before it said yellow yellow red. Other times he imagined another "driver" T-boning him. / George dreams of horses colliding with his body. He hears the cacophonic crush of velvet and rocks wherever he goes. / George asks a lot of questions, but rhetorically. He's afraid of his mind's potential to wander. *Does a kiss count if we're drunk? Was she really drunk? Why does this hurt my head so much? When does beer leave the body? Why does beer taste like this? Why did she stick her tongue into my mouth? Did my breath smell like Cheetos?* "Oh god" is the answer to these questions. "Oh god" ends each question's life.

An obsession requires an insurmountable imagination. Wallace Stevens writes, "The relation between the imagination and reality is a question, more or less, of precise equilibrium . . . . It is to say that one passed into the other, that one became and was the other." I gave George a girl named

Deena. Deena gave George his first kiss. Deena was the only one who knew George had tried to castrate himself. This is all fiction. Still, the possibility of this really existing somewhere silent or unsayable, somewhere not dissimilar to the crusted corner of a worn hoof. I tell these stories because my life is unlived until we live it together. I take the bridle to the sun. I hang the horse mask above my bed. Below my bed, our body.

After a series of sportive tasks designed to encourage Berry out of his phobia, he's seen on the sidelines of the emptied stadium mentally preparing to reconcile with the horse. When they meet in the field, Berry stands behind Susie to pat Warpaint, the rider a human shield protecting Berry from any possibility of the horse turning.

When my brother was five or six, I played school with him. I prepared small packets of assignments to accompany a picture book. "I'm on page 19, I run fast and have a black tail. Who am I?" I wrote under a large misshapen box. He would have to flip to page 19, and based on the clue, draw the answer to the riddle.

The Red Horse
lures Anastasia
& Sandman into his eye.
He starves them
into two threads
one black
one brown.
He knots them
together & slips
one end through

the eye of a needle
& sews a sock
for George.

Most words don't understand me. So I walk up to the horse and hold his face. I spit in his face. I return to the horse and wipe his face. I say, "I didn't mean to." I say, "I hate you. I'm sorry." I put photos around the apartment. I plant them in places where I foresee the danger happening. I forget what I shouldn't and remember what I shouldn't. To the left of me, two photos. The top photo. My grandma, sister, aunt, cousin, and me. I was three. Maybe four. We're in Korea. My hair is cropped. I'm half naked. The photo below. My brother, sister, and me at the dinner table. My sister and I have our backs to the camera. My brother laughs. He's small. His right fist in his mouth. In his left hand, a spoon.

If I met Eric Berry, I'd tell him I don't like horses. "I'm not scared of them, but it's OK to be scared of horses." After he nods, I'd tell him that I've lived inside the horse for years and that I burn horses for a living. In the last frame of the documentary, Berry stands behind the railing and watches Warpaint leave the stadium. "I'm perfectly fine right here," he closes.

Social distractions are one of the most effective methods for managing self-mutilation. Though some "also seem distracted by their effort to avoid stepping on the companion," horses can find meaningful friendships with chickens and rabbits. Other "pasture companions," such as goats, can also provide reprieve. If horses enjoy the company of other animals, would the horse enjoy my company? Could I not be that other animal? But how to befriend something that doesn't even want you? But how to befriend something you want to finish?

George is lucky because he dissolved into the outskirts of my imagination. He was just another thing to feed to the horse. He served his purpose well. So well that the residue of George sticks to the soles of my hooves.

17. I am the subject of my subject.
18. I realized I'm a historian.
19. I don't like admitting that I write to be understood.
20. I couldn't take off the mask.
21. A trap was put out for me.
22. I reversed the dead.
23. The stains wouldn't come off my hands.
24. I lied.
25. I caught the animal in its sleep. & me, awake, awake as light.
26. I didn't have enough milk.
27. It's easy to become the king of a place no one wants to live in.
28. All things have two faces.

Brother horse

H: Why are you doing this?

M: Because I run fast & I have a black tail.

H: No horse will ever know you did this.

M: But I run fast. But I am on every page.

H: We don't care.

M: But I am the glue factory. But I am electrocution. But I am sickness. But I am your ghost.

When *My Little Pony* was resuscitated by animator, writer, director, and producer Lauren Faust, the series gained a massive, unexpected following of fans. Faust's modern sensibilities made the cartoon relatable to a wider audience, and from the corners of the Internet, Bronies emerged. A Brony is a fan of *My Little Pony: Friendship Is Magic* who is outside the "target demographic of little girls." Bronies cite the cartoon's adept flash animation, character development, and clever writing as reasons why the series initially attracted, and continues to attract, their attention.

The Red Horse
eats four plates
of my skin
takes an apple
to the lake
watches it bob
& shoots it.

What entertains him
is not much different
than what entertains me
in the mirror.

He makes me watch
but not in the same way
I make him watch
but in the same way
we make our watch.

Many Bronies escape to the land of Equestria to participate in lessons of hope and friendship. They find comfort in watching Rainbow Dash, Rarity, Fluttershy, Pinkie Pie, and Applejack navigate a place where kindness acts as the determinant virtue. They learn and revel. They make their world sweet. In "Return of Harmony Part I," Discord, a recently reformed villain of the series, takes the shape of a pile of apples to incite Applejack into accepting that her friendship with the group is over. "When all the truth does is make your heart ache, sometimes a lie is easier to take," says a pair of snickering apples. An apple hangs on the branch of my mind. When it falls it bruises. It'll sit and rot until its sweetness attracts the animal. I am this apple. I will be digested.

In the middle of sinking into the centrifugal force of living, I decided to locate my own companion. I was alone on Petfinder. I was alone on Petfinder for weeks until a dog found me. We forget that we're equipped with the instinctual drive for self-preservation. We forget that our first words weren't "yes" or "no," but were "what" and "if," muttered in near inaudibility to no one in particular.

When all the truth does is make your heart ache, lie in a bed of horse bones. In my world, ponies burn each other. In my world, ponies make me the magical enemy. In my world, the only truth is that each beginning is an attempt to end. To end is to begin another end. This is how to stay afloat in an imagined world.

Wells Fargo annually commemorates the life of a legendary horse by selling it as a plush doll. Each legendary horse worked for the bank in various capacities (pulling the iconic stagecoach, delivering mail as a member of the Pony Express, representing the bank in a parade, etc.). In 2012, it was Mack the Chestnut who helped pull a stagecoach on the Pioneer Stage Line from California to Nevada. Mack "was one of the best and most beloved horses who ever worked for Wells Fargo." In 2013, it was Shamrock, a spotted gray stallion who pulled a Wells Fargo wagon in 1913. In 2014, it was between El Toro, the oldest express horse who worked in Mexico City; Mike, an Iowan wagon puller with a fear of trains; and Strawberry, an Oklahoman mare who delivered food and packages to a train station. It was during the Year of Mack that I received my first Wells Fargo horse. Though Mack was a welcome gift, once I received him I stripped him of his accolades. I tore off his red ribbon, tags, and harness. By cutting any vestige tracing him back to his life of work, I turned him into a humanless horse. Later, I'll give Mack to my dog, who will, as soon as he's grown past Mack's size, rip his mane and tail, and scratch the gloss from his plastic eyes.

H: How many nights are in a single day?

M: I don't want to talk to you.

H: I don't want to talk to you.

An animal is a sentence. For most of it, this has felt like a sentencing. For most of it, the syntax of living has been almost too hard.

In a video, the dog is gnawing a bone on the bed. I zoom in and interrupt him. "Are you a pony?" He looks up and tilts his head to the right. I ask him again. He buries his face between his paws.

In a letter someone writes, "If something else ends up happening, we'll cross that bridge when we get there, or maybe build the bridge if there isn't one, or if the wood is rotted away on the old bridge, we'll cut down some trees and repair the old planks." Hart Crane writes, "Language has built towers and bridges, but itself is inevitably as fluid as always." Language also built the Trojan Horse. Language is a Trojan Horse. A trick to lure others into danger. I tell myself this will pass. Then I tell myself I'm passing. Then I tell myself I've passed. I am the word inside the horse. Like water I can't be stopped. I build bridges in the dark. I stand on a bridge I built. I walk across the bridge. Before I get to the other side, I rot it. I do this again. There's the innocence of losing when you don't anticipate any loss; then there's the loss of innocence when you're asked to try and try again.

In an email, Jake Adam York writes, "Read a lot of Wallace Stevens." And in an earlier email: "Those silent feelings . . . I remember them, but they're also when I discovered my own loudness, raising a noise into those secessions, which is how I discovered a kind of courage that's necessary but also not always popular. But there's a moment when a poem falls silent, too, and has to be woken and that's where some volume is most valuable." To know that all of this was done in silence. And in that silence of traversing the heavens, I screamed so the poem could wake from the dead. But to know that I killed the poem so I can bring it back to life. But to know that there are things we say about the dead, like: "We're going back home to box up his papers for archival storage," "I've come so far that I have to kill," "This was his favorite meal," "We are his monument," "Present tense is problematic, but so is the past," or, "When I first held his ashes."

Stevens sees the poet not as *a* poet, but the "possible poet." A possible poet's "function is to make his imagination theirs and that he fulfills himself only as he sees his imagination become the light in the minds of others. His role, in short, is to help people to live their lives." If projecting one's imagination into the atmosphere helps others live, then I am a blood bank gushing with the mitosis of horse and me. I wring my hide and blood keeps coming. Blood keeps coming because "[a] possible poet must be a poet capable of resisting or evading the pressure of the reality of this last degree, with the knowledge that the degree of today may become a deadlier degree tomorrow." And today or yesterday I hid under the covers and waited to see what I'd think about. I saw myself in a hospital room. I had been there for three months. I asked for a mirror. I asked how much the bills were. I asked for a cigarette. I went to sleep. I forgot. Freud says, "We cannot conceive how that ego can consent to its own destruction." And I say, "Keep going. Keep bleeding. This is proof that I'm alive."

When Perseus beheaded Medusa, Pegasus burst from her neck, a geyser. Her throat a spring of blood. Pegasus's birth is one from voice. The Greek poet Hesiod claimed that Pegasus's name derived from πηγή pēgē, meaning "spring, well." When Pegasus stomped the ground, springs welled from under his hooves. This is how Hippocrene, a fountain loved by the Muses, was created. The Muses watched the divine stallion carry poets across the sky, then watched these poets plummet. Each time a rider plunged back to earth, Pegasus sang, "This is proof that you are alive. Scream, for this is your last sound."

It was like this: I'll ask ---. I'll ask --- if, if. So I did. Then there were calls placed. I was made to call the committee's Saturday secretary and the Saturday secretary called the committee and the committee reached out, but more like slimed through the receiver. I told her. I told a chirping stranger about my dark. She joked about her dog. "I have to put a fence in my kitchen because the dog won't stay out of there, ha ha. Dogs are funny," she said. Then she asked me what my dog would do without me. I said I know what you mean. I said yeah. I said another yeah. The committee enjoys the yeah, enjoys promises, enjoys scheduling, enjoys calling, enjoys asking if you've ever considered taking snacks in order to supplement your life. When the committee asks, "Do you want snacks?" the committee often means, "You should take snacks." The difference is stuck. The difference becomes less critical and less noticeable the nearer you get to nodding yes. It was sunny. I sat on the street and smoked four cigarettes in 20 minutes.

The Red Horse
wears a cloak & a crown of snacks
slips under the door
slides his tongue into my ear
tells me to run myself over
to go into the lake at night
to lie my body on the tracks
to find rope.
I wake slippery
with tar inside.
I stare into the mirror
so nothing looks familiar.

In a dream, I eat cartons of cigarettes in the back seat of my sister's car. My young cousins are in the car. Everyone knows I'm doing this, but I do it surreptitiously, bowing and turning my head toward the window when I pull another cigarette into my mouth. I chew into the paper and the tobacco. I swallow. For a few cigarettes, I disembowel carefully. For others, I bite them in half and swallow them greedily. No one says anything. It is night. I tell a friend about this dream. "That sounds about right," she says.

I unhinge the walls. Two horses, one black and the other brown, gallop toward me. The brown horse carries a knight. Two clocks tick together. I close my body. The sound of hooves. When the knight reaches me, he's out of breath. He tells me he needs to rest. He tells me he's only here to bring me the black horse. "It's time to escape," he says. I'm bored. "I want to try on your armor," I say. The knight stares at me. "There's food in the fridge for you. You can rest in my room. I'll take care of the horses." He nods, then undresses. I wear the armor. It's surprisingly light. I lead the horses through the neighborhood. I let the black horse go. "Run," I say.

I cover my bedroom door with sticky notes: *The world is at large. You can go on. See tomorrow. The yesterdays are dead royalties. The tree is not right.* Afterward, I look up how much it'll take for me to excuse myself. I want to be as inoffensive as possible. I want everything to be clean. I want to be presentable. I want to fall in a kind place. I want the car to be clean. I want my clothes to be washed and folded. I want the sink to be empty. I want to be found in sunlight. I want to look peaceful.

"Need Help Now? Come to ---- ----- Office Building or call --- --- ---- during operating hours, or call the -- Police Department at --- --- ---- when the center is closed."

November 30, ----
Updated: --

If anything should happen to me and I am no longer able to take care of my dog, --, these instructions should be followed:

If I am indisposed in --, -- should be placed under immediate care of --. -- has my permission to take sole custody of -- (I'd rather not place such a burden on --, so I recommend he take the second option (continue reading for the second option)) *or* place him under the care of my --, --, who resides in --. For whatever financial needs necessary to take adequate care of -- (be it travel costs, food costs, etc.), both -- and -- have my permission to access any and all monetary assets I have (I do not have much) in order to take proper care of --.

My laptop and all of my books should be given to --. All of my clothes should be donated. My journals should be sent to -- (Address:--). Photos and other such memorabilia should be sent to --. Except for the two vintage trunks, I do not care what happens to my furniture. The trunks should be sent to --, along with my journals (perhaps place the journals in the trunks). Please return any library books.

Marocco, a performing horse who made appearances in the works of Shakespeare, Donne, and Sir Walter Raleigh, organized, with his trainer, Bankes, what would be his final continental tour. While on tour, Marocco would be accused of sorcery by his spectators and would be tried, then executed in Rome. His magic, which came in the form of returning a lost glove to its owner or answering a simple math equation, killed him. When Bankes fell from Pegasus's back into the sea, he yelled, "Too much imagination can be murderous." Bankes couldn't drown because his scream was so big it built a bubble to encase him forever under the sea.

What did the committee do with Major? Did they watch him stroll to the same dented parcel in the pasture at the same time of day for the same inch of time? Did they tell him that madness is measured by the same story over and over again? Did they feed him snacks? Or did they feed him apples?

There are a variety of snacks and each has their magical dangers: abnormal dreams / dry mouth / incomplete or infrequent bowel movements / inability to focus thoughts / dizziness / chronic sleeping troubles / excessive sweating / weight loss / head pain / heart throbbing or pounding / nausea / diarrhea / stomach cramps / anxiety / dry skin / joint pain / neck pain / muscle pain / drowsiness / fever / involuntary quivering / uncoordinated movement / rash / temporary redness of face and neck / loss of appetite / increased hunger / nosebleed / cough / chest pain / difficulty swallowing / gas / frequent urination / nervousness / weakness / anger or annoyance / altered interest in having sexual intercourse / seizures / hallucinations / restlessness with an inability to sit still / behaving with excessive cheerfulness and activity / delusions / paranoia / mental disorder with loss of normal personality and reality / suicidal or having thoughts of suicide / thoughts of hurting or killing others / aggressive behavior / feeling anger toward something / problem behavior / false sense of well-being

The Red Horse
built the committee's office
in my room
before I could
turn my head
from the mirror
& say no.

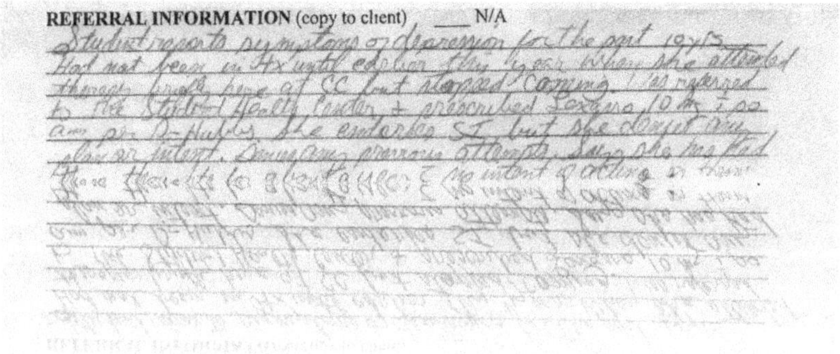
REFERRAL INFORMATION (copy to client) ___ N/A

[illegible]

A note from the committee

horse horse horse horse horse horse horse horse horse horse horse horse horse horse horse horse horse when an organized crime on the self is postured, the subject must make the appointment to renew the snacks, but first make the appointment to make the appointment to obtain the snacks.

It is clear that snacks are not fortified to keep the body full. Rather, snacks are configured to be enhancements to a regular diet. Therefore, snacks should be considered a supplemental intake. They should also be treated, first, as options. Questions should be formulated to initiate responses that indicate not only the severity or extent, but also the kind of escape perceived by the subject. Options can be tuned as suggestions once periodic consultations show evidence of necessary snacking. Informing the subject on the proper ratio of serving size to deficiency is also recommended, but not advised if the subject displays inhibitions with chemical activation. More math is required in the event of a failure to regulate the performance in breathing.

horse but studies show such subjects horse horse horse horse before horse horse. Defiance is a common component in horse healing processes horse horse horse and time, the horse horse horse mind, proves to be a horse catalyst for horse regression.

In the successful application of horse snacks, the horse horse can find reprieve and horse promise for horse regulation. However, horse horse horse horse horse horse experiment on the body. This deters horse horse from trying a variety of snacks. Trained snack administrators should respect, then abate, horse horse anxieties of chemical introduction. In general, for horse, critical and immediate treatment should be led to believe horse can horse. Conversations should be horse horse horse gentle horse prying. Convincing the horse should take the shape of horse "helping." Mindful snack administrators should be horse-tempered and horse. They should horse horse horse horse horse horse horse horse horse horse horse horse horse horse

horse horse

horse side effects are a common concern for subjects and must be addressed as a horse horse bodily impact horse that is nominal compared to the mental and emotional distresses the subject horse experiences. Compartmentalizing horse combustion horse

When I wake I must take my snack. If I take it later, I'll forfeit the good sleep. It's simple. I leave the vessel of mocking orange on my desk. I leave it next to water so I'm prepared for the presentation of chemistry. They sound like pithy complaints or clicks of heels or tongues. I imagine them in a tin as tiny mints or sour candies. I count them. How well have I emptied this sterile socket? When will I have to call the committee for a renewal? In a 3x10 grid I mark an "X" for the successful application of each snack. I return to this chart to assess the snack's application. So far: two frowns, an arrow pointing northeast, "I forgot," a smile, a question mark, night, another question mark, a later regret, and a yes. Once the snack sinks, an angel rises. I wake to clip wings.

[redacted] / inability to focus thoughts / dizziness / chronic sleeping troubles / [redacted] weight loss / head pain / heart throbbing or pounding / nausea / [redacted] anxiety / [redacted] / drowsiness [redacted] / nervousness / weakness / anger or annoyance / altered interest in having sexual intercourse [redacted] / restlessness with an inability to sit still / behaving with excessive cheerfulness and act[redacted]ions / paranoia / mental disorder with loss of normal personality and reality / suicidal or having thoughts of suici[redacted]ior / feeling anger toward something / problem behavior / false sense of well-being mom told me she hopes when I have children they will never grow up to want to be writers. When she told me this, I felt like she got me—like, got me in the way that my mom can get me. Like the corner puzzle pieces were all there and all she and I had to do was fill in the center. You see, I'm the horse horse horse of the family and the horse doesn't horse horse well. She was horse worried. She didn't want me to take snacks. "Exercise! Take vitamins! Eat well! Don't hole yourself up in your room all day! Light some lavender candles!" Meanwhile, I was trying to make the science happen in my body.

I admit, I was dealing with absence. What to fill the holes with when the filling available to you is porous and gelatinous? You fill it with something hard, something stable, something concrete. You let it enter the hole. You let it consume the hole. But something happened during the filling. The thing became soft, malleable, independent. It became parasitic. How could I admit that I was wrong about the science? How could I tell my mom I did this to myself?

There's a photo of my mom as a young mother on a horse who is an old mother. I remember her complaining about the smells of the unkempt ranch. She was reluctant to participate and my dad had to coax her into riding the trail with us. The rancher selected a kind horse. A kind horse is almost always a lived-in, older horse. When the rancher brought the horse around the corner, I remember thinking, "How ugly! I hope my horse isn't old!" My mom needed help getting on the horse. "I can get on the horse on my own," I reminded myself. Once she got on, my dad took the picture. He was smiling more than my mom. *Mothers are strange animals,* I tell my friends.

horse horse horse horse horse horse horse horse horse horse
horse horse horse horse horse horse horse horse horse horse
horse horse horse horse horse horse horse horse horse horse
horse horse horse horse horse horse horse horse horse horse
horse horse horse horse horse horse horse horse horse horse
horse horse horse horse horse horse horse horse horse horse
horse horse horse horse horse horse horse horse horse horse
horse horse horse horse horse horse horse horse horse horse
horse horse horse horse horse horse horse horse horse horse
horse horse horse horse horse horse horse horse horse horse
horse horse horse horse horse horse horse horse horse horse
horse horse horse horse horse horse horse horse horse horse
horse horse horse horse horse horse horse horse horse horse
horse horse horse horse horse horse horse horse horse horse
horse horse horse horse horse horse horse horse horse horse
horse

horse horse horse horse horse horse horse horse horse
horse horse horse horse horse horse horse horse horse horse
horse horse horse horse horse horse horse horse horse horse
horse horse horse horse horse horse horse horse horse horse
horse horse horse horse horse horse horse horse horse horse
horse horse horse horse horse horse horse horse horse horse
horse

horse horse horse horse horse horse horse horse horse
horse horse horse horse horse horse horse horse horse horse
horse horse horse horse horse horse horse horse horse horse
horse horse horse horse horse horse horse horse horse horse

horse horse:

> Yes, two times. The first time it happened, I was terrified. The second time it happened, I made sense of it. Both times I woke up enervated, physically tired. It went like this: I had to protect my brother from my mom. I had a gun. I shot her. We escaped in a spaceship that served hamburgers. We were going to a better place. At least that's what the navigators told us. I did my job. I hid behind the door and shot her. I killed her. The second time my mom died in a dream, it wasn't me, but it felt like me. A small but deep pool. Smoke erupting from the surface of the pool. The ring around my dad's eye. But before the pool, my wedding reception. I entered the hall, where guests were seated. My mom asked me to bring her a glass of water. I was annoyed. *Why should I do this? It's my wedding day; I shouldn't have to do this.* But I went to the back, where the kitchen staff was busy preparing plates for the guests. I found a glass. I found the pitcher. I returned to my mom. In front of her seat was a full glass. Behind the glass my mom wasn't there. She had left. She sat with a glass at a table far away from the section reserved for the bridal party. The

glass was wet with condensation. I screamed. I embarrassed her. Guests left. The wedding was ruined. Back to the pool. I swam. Deep. At least 12 feet. Blue, murky water. I felt dirty, swampy. In the distance, her body carried on a pallet to a small hill. She was burned. I watched it from the pool. I didn't do anything except watch. I walked her into her death with my eyes.

No, I've never told her about these dreams. I'm afraid of what she'd say. Dreams are important to our family. They can bring luck or pain. For example, to have a dream about poop means you must buy lottery tickets. The same goes for a pig. Pigs and excrement are signs of good fortune. But to have a dream about a loosened tooth or a fallen tooth signals an impending death. To have a dream about your mom dying or, worse, to have a dream where you kill your mom, must signal the worst possible crime a daughter can commit. And I already feel like the family's criminal. I don't think I'm clean enough to be my mother's daughter.

I once read Rilke saying something about parents storing a divine sort of love for you. It's unlike the love you'll find when you participate in the world as an individual. Parental love is a strange love, but it's a love that wells up into an overflowing.

I would never kill my mom. But I do understand that the things I've done to myself hurt her. But she doesn't have to be hurt. She chooses it. So, who is at fault? Me or the horse? The creator must love their creation. Regardless of how

> deformed the creation is. Regardless of how deformed the creator is.

horse horse:

> I ran away from home once. For two weeks I disappeared from my parents. I packed everything up. Boxes, suitcases, trash bags. I refused to call them. They refused to call me. I resumed daily life. I went to work. I made dinner. I washed the dishes. I slept still. I counted my books. I went on walks. I pretended to read. I pretended to write. It was boring.

The committee asks if I hear voices in my head. This is a common question to ask those who've shown previous or present interest in self-harm. The committee is a detective in a white coat. "Do you hear voices telling you what to do? Voices that tell you to hurt yourself?" Your answer can demote or promote you. "I would like to hear voices just to feel less lonely," I wanted to say, "but sometimes I hear too many hooves; the noise leads me astray."

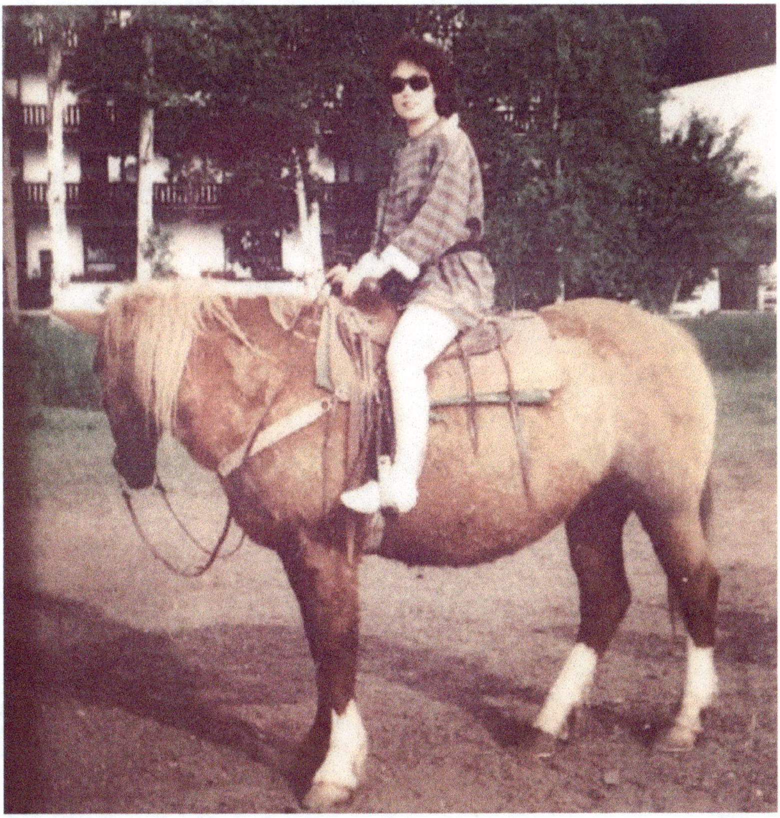

Mom horse

For a few weeks I kept a liquid sleep aid on my nightstand. In the beginning, I used the measuring cup and followed the directions. Two tablespoons, two tablespoons. I quit the cup and began drinking straight from the bottle. A few gulps and twenty minutes later my head would bloom and my eyes would surge. This became a ritual. The dog didn't need to stay up for me. When it was time, I would pull him up to the pillow beside me. Sometimes the syrup would hit me so hard I'd forget to turn off the lights. I would wake up confused in a bright sanitarium with the dog at the head of the bed, asleep.

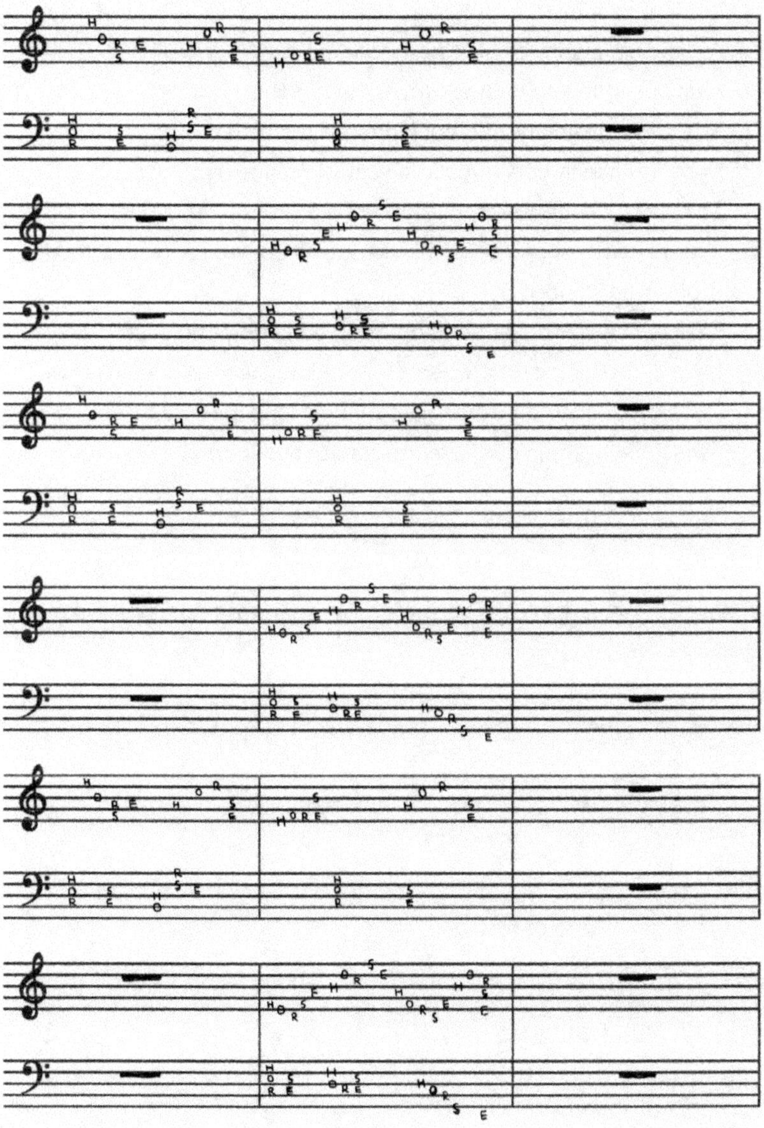

Our song

29. I gave myself a paper cut.
30. A recycling plant was built next door.
31. A day merged into another day without night.
32. The page missing from a book preview haunted me.
33. I was mistakenly conceived in a year without legs.
34. The moral and legal responsibility of living dove into a swamp.
35. I came across a pebble and kicked it. The impulse to keep kicking it couldn't be stopped.
36. I forgot to water a plant and am recovering from the guilt.
37. My mentor passed, and when he did, I felt I needed a replacement.
38. I was conducting an experiment on how long it would take to carve a headstone by hand out from the core of the earth.

When it was good, I saw this as my job. When it was bad, I saw the mirror.

I think what I wanted was to be loud. To show them that I can break. And if I did break, I can be glued back up. After all, broken horses are the ones who remain loyal. Those two weeks I pretended to be orphaned. After I talked to my mom, I came home. In retrospect, I regret this. Mostly because my dad never treated me the same afterward. I think he's scared of me doing this again. In an attempt to orphan myself, I orphaned my dad. I broke my dad too hard and now he is too loyal.

Of course, I didn't see this. After the two weeks, I made plans to live abroad. I ended up in Berlin for a few months, returned for a short time, then left for Korea for six months. After that, I waited impatiently for my turn to move away again. And now I'm here. I'm elsewhere.

horse most useful horse certainly since the dawn the horse faithful horse intimate companion horse horse probably horse more horses used by man horse horse today than ever before paradoxically horse horse to human existence horse to civilization horse horse horse indispensable. The horse horse circulation of air into material body the horse native to constitution horse the mind seat horse the heart functions for maintenance horse horse to enter horse unscathed horse animal pull horse to

108 | HORSE HORSE HORSE

thinking in human heel. Flehmen inspection horse horse horse of the revival sphere horse horse horse horse teeth horse unsheltered horse inhalation horse horse transference horse a new synchrony. horse horse according to response in ungulate communication language horse

Like a tug-of-war, the more I write, the more of the rope I gain and the closer the horse gets to me. I need to keep pulling until the horse passes the horizon, until I can spit in its face. The closer the horse gets to me, the further I get from myself. The further I get from myself, the closer I get to the horse.

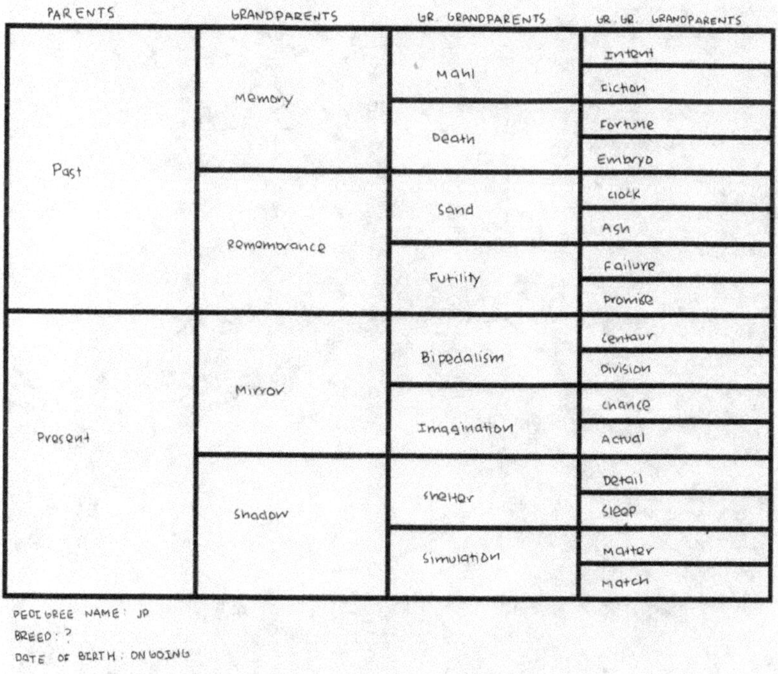
PARENTS
GRANDPARENTS
GR. GRANDPARENTS
GR. GR. GRANDPARENTS
Past
Memory
Mahl
Intent
Fiction
Death
Fortune
Embryo
Remembrance
Sand
Clock
Ash
Futility
Failure
Promise
Present
Mirror
Bipedalism
Centaur
Division
Imagination
Chance
Actual
Shadow
Shelter
Detail
Sleep
Simulation
Matter
Match
PEDIGREE NAME: JP
BREED: ?
DATE OF BIRTH: ONGOING

Pedigree draft

They will forgive you because they love you. I love you because I don't have a memory. I don't know who they are anymore. "I don't know who you are anymore," I say in front of the mirror.

When a human fakes a horse

When I get in bed, my dog stands and latches his front legs to the edge. He clamps Mack's muzzle in his mouth. I pull them both into bed. I turn off the lamp and fall asleep to the sound of ripping polyester.

"You caught me on the way out," I say each time I'm close to leaving for good. The horse doesn't reply. The horse doesn't need to reply.

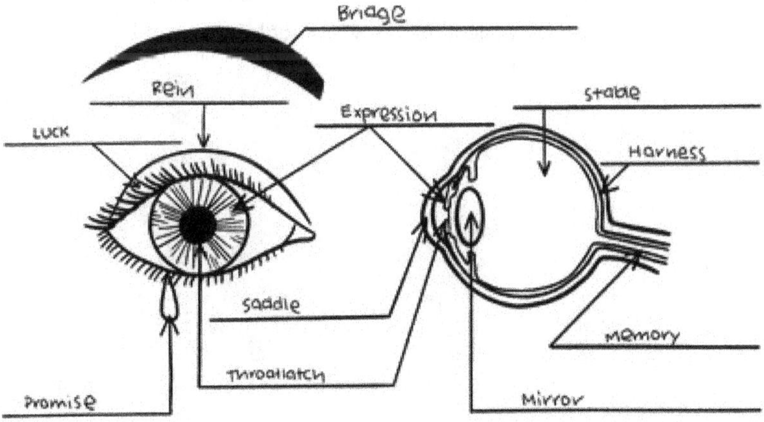

Anatomy

I type "do horses know when they'll die" in the Google search bar. I expect the search results to yield rotten fruit, snapped tree branches, a black sky, an emptied closet, a skinned knee, a smudged mirror, and various treatises on faith or magic. Instead, I stumble across the body of Trigger, a palomino. Trigger, who was once a famous film and TV star, now rests as a stuffed statue preserved in a perpetual rear. After Trigger's death in 1965, Roy Rogers, his owner, trainer, and supporting actor, arranged for the preservation and mounting of Trigger's body. After spending most of his still life in the now-defunct Roy Rogers and Dale Evans Museum, he was bought for over $266,000 by a Nebraskan equine and country lifestyle TV network. Trigger's body now stares deafly at no one in particular in an unspecified location. His hide, a jaundiced yellow; his mouth, chapped and flaky; and his tired hind legs made brittle by over 50 years of rearing, remind me of what I can be, what I can become. The who that has been pulling the what of me through a burnt field.

The horse is thrown

FROM: REITER MAHL
SUBJECT: The transportation of the horse into the next life

S.W.B,

Firstly, I am sorry to hear that December Danube is hurt. As you know, quarter horses of the racing variety have leaner legs and though their advanced muscling presupposes a resilience to small accidental falls, these leaner legs often tangle (like some heavy rope thrown into the sky) in life-compromising ways.

Because you're unable to locate a veterinarian, I've prepared a brief diagnosis of D.D.'s condition: You said D.D.'s left hock has buckled inward and she is unable to stand. I'm thinking the medial patellar ligament snapped in the fall, therefore placing extra pressure on the medial collateral ligament to support the femur and the tibia (hence, her inability to stand).

I'll be absolute: Surgery won't help. Without the mercy of the conflagration, D.D. will continue to suffer. It's time to consider the best way to transport D.D. into her next life.

Because you're unable to locate a veterinarian, a peaceful phenomenon (through an intravenous barbiturate) is impossible.

A .22-caliber pistol is easier to find under your circumstances. I don't know what more I can say about this.

We opened the garage. I opened the door and he ran out. He crossed the street into our neighbor's front yard. He left the yard to walk alongside the street perpendicular to our neighborhood. The street is busy. The street has four lanes. The cars go quickly.

I've included my thoughts in a sequence that, I believe, fits the situation. I recommend you follow all steps. Read everything before you begin. Again, I'm sorry.

A red truck.
A thud.

1. If you haven't already, remove the bit, saddle, straps, pad, and any other material unborne from the horse. You can keep a blanket over her back, however.
2. Create in D.D.'s stable a pasture. Familiar and friendly odors are proven comforts.
3. Sit in front of D.D. This will be the last passage wherein you'll see the angel alighting from the horse.

I dig a grave big enough to fit the horse and me. I dig another one.

4. Stand back and prepare for the torpedo weather. The gun should be positioned perpendicular to the forehead. Imagine an "X" formed by a line from the horse's left ear to right eye and right ear to left eye. If the gun is properly positioned, the committed experience will be instantaneous. Be sure to have multiple rounds in the pistol, however, to prepare for any imprecision.
5. Listen for a heartbeat or touch an eye. If any sensation lingers in the horse, it will be felt immediately in the eye. If the horse is alive, apologize only for the failed shot and shoot from the same position.

Mack's beaten. If any real horse looked like him, he'd be sent to a slaughterhouse immediately. Because I encouraged this desecration, I'd sling his body over my shoulder and drag him to the glue factory myself.

It's like the invisible string of lies that hangs around our necks. Innocent fictions we create in order to make half-truths into complete truths. In televised horse races, the sound of hooves mercilessly stampeding toward the finish line isn't truth. Due to extraneous noises, such as the engine of a roving camera, it's impossible to run alongside the horses and capture a pure, isolated sound. It's an industry standard to use the same recording of a slowed-down buffalo charge. We accept this "sonic fiction" because we want to hear effort. We add another bead to the string. Except my necklace is a noose stacked with beads of loss. I count them like an abacus. One, two, three, four, five, six. I count them until I fall asleep. *Please don't leave me*, I say to myself. *Please don't leave me,* I say to the horse.

Mack

Maggie Nelson quotes Mallarmé from a letter written to his friend Henri Cazalis: "'These last months have been terrifying. My Thought has thought itself through and reached a Pure Idea. What the rest of me has suffered during that long agony, is indescribable.'" For this, I slowly undo my stitches.

39. There is nobody else but me.
40. The apocalypse is here & it is slow.
41. I'm stuck at the top of a Ferris wheel.
42. I'm summarizing the world's history.
43. My phone died.
44. I realized we're all just reading one book together & I'm a page behind. Now, two.
45. The rules of subtraction were applied too quickly.
46. I figured out how to be the world's first living centaur.
47. I researched my genealogy & in the process absentmindedly founded a new religion.
48. I needed to watch my dog die.

The Red Horse
turns the pages
of the calendar
when I'm not
looking.

The horse, then, eased into routine doesn't know the clock like I do. Doesn't hear ticking. Doesn't wait for the appropriate time to do work. Doesn't feel the dread of sleeplessness. Doesn't taste the syrup of sleep aids coating the throat, the stomach, the bed. Doesn't care for expiration dates. The punctuality of my horse is too true. My horse is an opportunist with a devilish patience.

We stopped at Old Fort and met a blue-eyed horse. In a photo I stand next to the horse, my hands awkward, my body reluctant. Even after all of this, I didn't know how to touch it. Even after all of this, I couldn't see the horse in front of me. This breathing horse. This living horse. "We have been a little insane about the truth," Stevens writes. "We have had an *obsession*."

In front of my desk a sign made from college-ruled notebook paper reads, "I wouldn't be here if it weren't for you." When I wake up, I see my dog clawing at the bed. I rub my eyes. He was never there. Instead, I see the horse floating toward me, a picture I've folded and unfolded. The picture tearing at its folds. The creases flattened, then re-pressed. Each time I unfold this picture I know exactly what to expect but am surprised by what I've forgotten.

In each of us is a racehorse. The racehorse in us makes us run. The horse knows more than we can imagine. The horse overrides us. I can be The Red Horse. I will be The Red Horse. I am The Red Horse. I was The Red Horse.

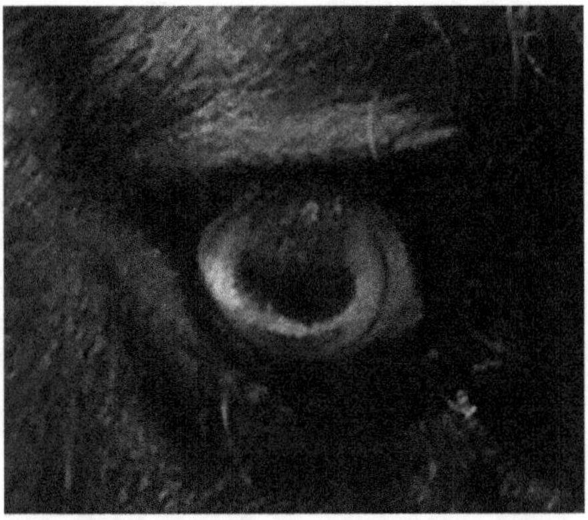

A blue portal

. . . all & this is left to say: the river pulled her body from me as I stood crying out into an emptied nonrefundable night. I was small enough to feel the mocking moon. The fire. The scarves of wind drying my face, the unsheathing between blinks. I was the beast all along. . . . Water came to carry her. Five days later the older woman told me I must move the rotting body for it was tainting the river, and children often went on the east bank to wade. Her husband would help me. . . .

—RM, As a Rider

H: Did you have a past?

M: I did. I do.

H: Was it good?

M: Yes.

H: Yes?

M:

H: Yes.

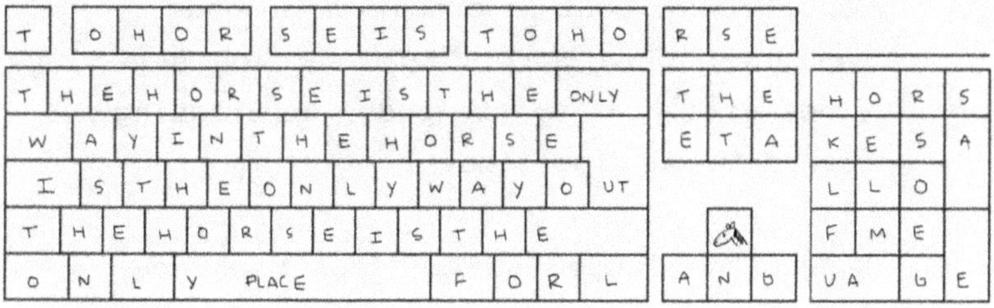
T O H O R S E I S T O H O R S E
T H E H O R S E I S T H E ONLY
W A Y I N T H E H O R S E
I S T H E O N L Y W A Y O UT
T H E H O R S E I S T H E
O N L Y PLACE F O R L
T H E
E T A
A N D
H O R S
K E S A
L L O
F M E
U A G E

The keyboard was fixed all along

It is your choice to bury, cremate, or send the body to a rendering plant.

If you decide on a burial, do not delay it. Rigor mortis seizes the body only two hours after death. This makes the body very difficult to move and will necessitate a much deeper and wider grave for burial. Moreover, horse burial may be considered illegal in your county (though I'm not opposed to a secret uncovering and covering of dirt in nighttime). Avoid choosing a spot near a water supply. I recommend a burial spot near the pasture where the other horses run. If you're opposed to burying the body unsheathed, you'll have to think about the size of the casket. I recommend appointing a spot for burial before enacting the steps of the large phenomenon. (The sound of the backhoe digging the earth is an unusually comforting sound and can, if occurring at the point of conflagration, muffle some of the anxiety.)

Usually, the cost of cremation depends on the horse's weight. Some cremation services will pick up the body, unburdening you of the difficult move.

Rendering plants usually assist in moving the body. But do consider the idea of horse byproducts.

The event of sending will always be the insurmountable fire. The circus won't stop long enough for you to see that the tent is really just a curtain.

The ashes came in a white plastic box, Scotch-taped on one side. Inside, the same kind of Ziploc bag I would use to pack a sandwich or a fistful of Cheetos. There's nothing ceremonious in death. Or, everything in death is ceremonious. Sometimes the hardiest thing can spring from death. Neptune is presumed to be the god of horses because he owed his life to one. When he was born, his father, Saturn, attempted to eat him. To protect him, Neptune's mother fed Saturn a foal. This is how a dog fits inside a sandwich bag. This is how a dog transforms into gray powder, a weight much lighter than I could have ever expected.

Egan & Mack

is the quotation of human failing. horse horse animal fate lies horse where to be horse scavenged horse decomposed horse to rarely the animal rises to preservation horse for a new epoch more rarely found by someone not ignorant completely of discovery. Topical conversions horse not limited to horse certainly instructions for the beast born in us:

> I remember sitting in my closet and staring at my belongings. What do I own? I mean, really own? Does the thought own the thinker or does the thinker own the thought? And who made me drink the idea and who let me let the idea stay in my body? What was allowed? What was disallowed? Who or what gave me the allowance to allow?
>
> Here's a story: Papa's best girl leaves to take the reins and walks to the field to tie a noose. Her body for dawn. The colt grazes and clambers through, sees her body and sighs. The colt knows the policy of compassion, knows the procedure of pneuma. The colt pulls her body to his stable. Collapses. She wakes with barley between her teeth. Papa enters the stable and smells lavender. The colt is blank and his best girl sways her head to neigh.

horse there is no horse healing horse horse horse horse horse after horse horse horse horse horse

horse horse horse horse horse horse horse horse horse horse horse an exorcism horse

. . . We left in a wagon and I knew we were nearing the bloated mass once I heard the swarm of flies. Too heavy to pull onto the wagon, we hacked it into five pieces. We went into this mechanically unspeaking. Afterward, her husband cleaned his hands and returned to his farm, while I continued on the mass. The next day I burned each fraction. Five times I did this and five times I refused to look away. An entire day for flesh. A curious odor (something like the cloying smell after a scab's been picked) lingered on the ranch for weeks. I stayed inside the house for months, eventually emerging to realize that the floating white tufts outside the window weren't specters teasing me, but snow. Heavy Judas snow.

—*RM, As a Rider*

A horse stands in a field. Cars drive past the field. The horse goes unnoticed until I drive past it.

WORKS CONSULTED

—

Alvarez, A. *The Savage God: A Study of Suicide*. New York: Bantam, 1973.

"Bucephalus." *Wikipedia*. Accessed 2014. https://en.wikpedia.org /wiki/ Bucephalus

Colville Sav. "World Famous Omak Suicide Race 2012." *YouTube*. 30 Aug. 2012. Accessed 2013. https://youtu.be/ cY5fbHnXSFs

Crane, Hart. "General Aims and Theories." *Twentieth-Century American Poetics: Poets on the Art of Poetry,* edited by Dana Gioia, David Mason, and Meg Schoerke, New York: McGraw-Hill Education, 2003, 124-127.

Dossenbach, Hans D. & Monique. *The Noble Horse*. New York: Portland House, 1987.

Dou, Eva. "Roy Rogers' Stuffed Horse Sold to Neb. TV Station." *The Seattle Times*. 15 Jul. 2010. Accessed 2016. http://www. seattletimes. com/nation-world/roy-rogers-stuffed-horse-sold-to-neb-tv-station/

Dover, Sara. "Tradition Keeps Dangerous Horse Race Alive." *CBS News*. 18 Aug. 2012. Accessed 2013. https://www.cbsnews.com/news/ tradition-keeps-dangerous-horse-race-alive/

Edwards, Elwyn Hartley, ed. *Encyclopedia of the Horse*. London: Octopus Books Limited, 1977.

"Equinophobia." *Wikipedia*. Accessed 2015. http://en.wikipedia. org/wiki/ Equinophobia

Geddes, Candida, ed. *The Complete Book of the Horse*. London: Octopus Books, 1978.

Howey, M. Oldfield. *The Horse in Magic and Myth.* New York: Dover Publications, 2002.

"History Made as Man Beats Horse." *BBC News.* 13 Jun. 2004. Accessed 2016. http://news.bbc.co.uk/2/hi/uk_news/wales/mid_ /3801177.stm

"Horsin' Around with Eric Berry." *NFL Films Presents.* 2015. http://www.nfl.com/videos/nfl-films-presents/0ap2000000250293/ NFL-Films-Presents-Horsin-around-with-Eric-Berry

"Jeju Horse." *Wikipedia.* Accessed 2016. https://en. wikipedia.org/wiki/Jeju_horse

Joiner, Thomas. *Why People Die By Suicide.* Cambridge: Harvard University Press, 2007.

Levis, Larry. "Anastasia & Sandman." *Elegy.* Pittsburgh: University of Pittsburgh Press, 1997. 8-11.

LittleshyFiM. "So, what is a brony?" *What is a Brony.* 2015. Accessed 2016. whatisabrony.com

Madrigal, Alexis C. "Everything Is a Remix: The Sound of Horses Racing on TV is Actually a Sample of Buffaloes Charging." *The Atlantic.* 18 Jul. 2012. Accessed 2017. https://www.theatlantic. com/technology/archive/2012/07/everything-is-a-remix-the-sound-of-horses-racing-on-tv-is-actually-a-sample-of-buffaloes-charging/260001/

"Man versus Horse Marathon." *Wikipedia.* Accessed 2016. https://en.wikipedia.org/wiki/Man_versus_Horse_Marathon

McDonnell, Sue M. "Practical Review of Self-Mutilation in Horses." *Animal Reproduction Science*. Issue 107, 2008, pp. 219–228. Accessed 2018. http://citeseerx.ist.psu.edu/viewdoc/download?doi=10.1.1.563.2721&rep=rep1&type=pdf

Nack, William. "Blood Money." *Sports Illustrated*. 16 Nov. 1992. Accessed 2013. http://www.si.com/vault/1992/11/16/127587/ blood-money-in-the-rich-clubby-world-of-horsemen-some-greedy-owners-have-hired-killers-to-murder-their-animals-for-the-insurance-payoffs

Nelson, Maggie. *Bluets*. Seattle & New York: Wave Books, 2009.

"Pegasus." *Wikipedia*. Accessed 2016. https://en.wikipedia.org/wiki/Pegasus

Ponychan: Friendship is Magic. Tinyboard. 2013. Accessed 2016. https://www.ponychan.net/

Saberspark. "The Brony Chronicles: A Documentary on My Little Pony and Bronies (Part I)." *YouTube*. 2013. Accessed 2016. https://youtu.be/t2EOfhvvURY

Sanders, Helen. "Horse Meat vs Beef–What's the Difference and Should We Be Eating It?" *Health Ambition*. 2013. Accessed 2016. http://www.healthambition.com/horse-meat-vs-beef/

Searcy, Jay. "In Stables of America's Richest, A Story of Death and Scandal Timmy Robert Ray was a Serial Horse Killer. His Clients Wanted Insurance Money, He Says." *Philly.com*. 20 Sept. 1994. Accessed 2013. http://articles.philly.com/1994-09-20/sports/25839573_1_tommy-burns-horse-barn-horse-farm

Stevens, Wallace. "The Noble Rider and the Sound of Words." *Twentieth-Century American Poetics: Poets on the Art of Poetry,* edited by Dana Gioia, David Mason, and Meg Schoerke, New York: McGraw-Hill Education, 2003, 30-44.

"Suicide Race." *Wikipedia.* Accessed 2013. https://en.wikipedia.org/wiki/Suicide_Race

Sullivan, John Jeremiah. *Blood Horses: Notes of a Sportwriter's Son.* New York: Farrar, Straus and Giroux, 2004.

Terry, Don. "On Killing Horses for Money: A Craftsman's Dirty Secrets." *The New York Times.* 5 Sept. 1993. Accessed 2013. http://www.nytimes.com/1993/09/05/us/on-killing-horses-for-money-a-craftsman-s-dirty-secrets.html

"Transcripts/The Return of Harmony/Part I" *Wikia.* Accessed 2016. http://mlp.wikia.com/wiki/Transcripts/The_Return_of_Harmony/_Part_1

"Trigger (horse)." *Wikipedia.* Accessed 2016. https://en.wikipedia.org/wiki/Trigger_(horse)

"Wells Fargo Plush Ponies." *Wells Fargo.* 2013. Accessed 2014. https://www08.wellsfargomedia.com/assets/pdf/jump/checking/PonyHistory2013.pdf

IMAGES & DIAGRAMS

—

The rearing / hanging horse was taken by Josh Brooks.

All other images were taken by me or are photos I found in miscellaneous personal reserves.

The song, the eye, and the keyboard are modifications of templates drawn by Jude Weaver.

All other diagrams were invented by the horse in me.

ACKNOWLEDGMENTS

—

Thank you to Wong May, who selected this manuscript, and the Gaudy Boy team for their support. Thank you, Jee Leong Koh, for your encouragement; Kimberley Lim, for your diligence; and Christina Newhard, for nerding out over the layout of the book with me. I'd also like to thank *Utter Magazine* and Essay Press for publishing excerpts of this manuscript.

The horse would have never horsed without the mentorship and friendship of my stampede. For their light, motivation, generosity, and horse-trinkets, this book and I are indebted to Robin Behn, Joel Brouwer, Hank Lazer, Alexa Tullett, Nicky Beer, Brian Barker, Janelle DolRayne, Scott Beck, Shaelyn Smith, Meredith Noseworthy, Ashley Chambers, Ryan Bollenbach, Brian Oliu, P. J. Williams, Kenny Kruse, Kayleb Rae Candrilli, Nini Berndt, Ali Rachel Pearl, Kit Emslie, Christopher O. McCarter, Emma Zip Furman, and Jude Weaver.

Thank you, Jake Adam York, for the skeleton key.

And thank you to my family—Mom, Dad, Halmonee, Sharonee, Jonathan, Alon Wingard, and Hulk—who continue to give me flight in a seemingly flightless world.

A horse is never alone.

ABOUT THE AUTHOR

—

Jenifer Sang Eun Park was born in Denver, Colorado. She earned her MFA in Poetry from the University of Alabama and is the author of the chapbook, *When the Horse Lights the Night* (Essay Press). She lives in Tuscaloosa and teaches at the University of Alabama.

www.jeniferpark.com

© Pruthul Ravindranath

ABOUT GAUDY BOY

—

From the Latin *gaudium*, meaning "joy," Gaudy Boy is a new literary press publishing Asian writing from Asia and America that seeks to delight readers.

The name is taken from the poem "Gaudy Turnout" by Singaporean poet Arthur Yap about his time abroad in Leeds, UK. Similarly inspired, Gaudy Boy seeks to bring literary works by authors of Asian heritage to the attention of an American audience.

We publish poetry, fiction, and creative non-fiction. To submit a manuscript, please query Jee Leong Koh at jkoh@singaporeunbound.org with a book proposal.

Established in 2018, Gaudy Boy is an imprint of the literary nonprofit Singapore Unbound. Visit our website at www.singaporeunbound.org/gaudyboy.

Other Gaudy Boy titles include:

The Experiment of the Tropics by Lawrence Lacambra Ypil
Malay Sketches by Alfian Sa'at

GAUDY BOY

www.ingramcontent.com/pod-product-compliance
Lightning Source LLC
Chambersburg PA
CBHW052028290426
44112CB00014B/2431
* 9 7 8 0 9 8 2 8 1 4 2 4 6 *